D1265958

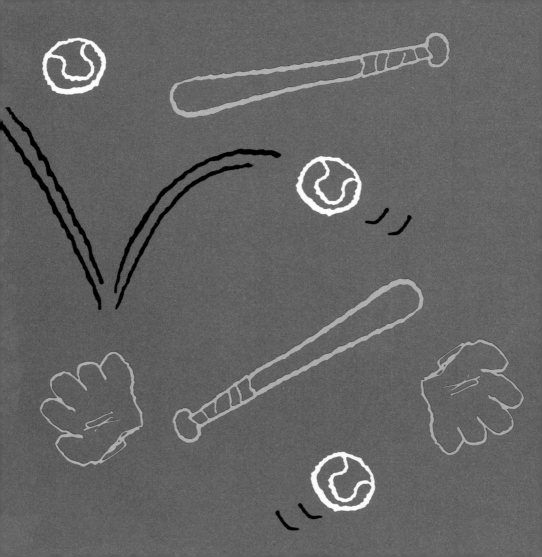

On And Off The Field

by

Schulz

KONECKY&KONECKY

Konecky & Konecky LLC
72 Ayers Point Road
Old Saybrook, CT 06475
www.koneckyandkonecky.com

ISBN: 1-56852-767-5

Printed and bound in Hong Kong

Insights From The Outfield

To Mary~
Happy Birth day
to you~ this book
especially for you because
you're the best sports
fan ever ~ especially
when it comes to the
grandkids' games!
Enjoy!
L.J. & Joni
7-13-2011

The
Dream Team

The Dream Team

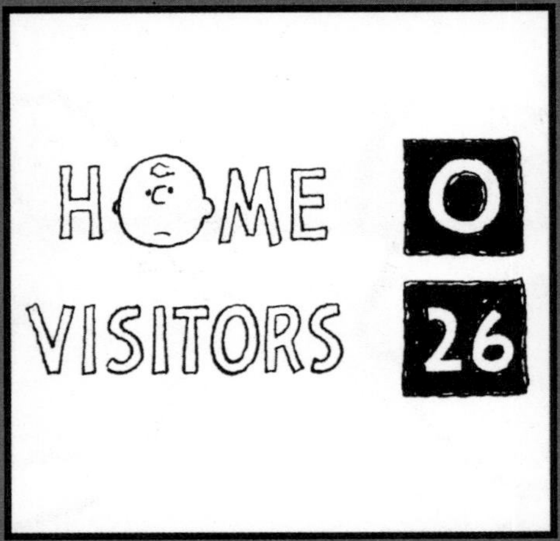
HOME 0
VISITORS 26

It's How You Play The Game

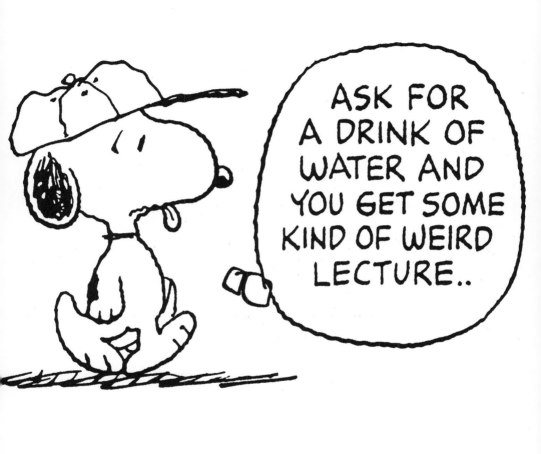

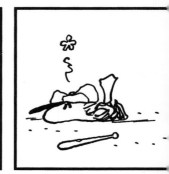

Memoirs
From The
Mound

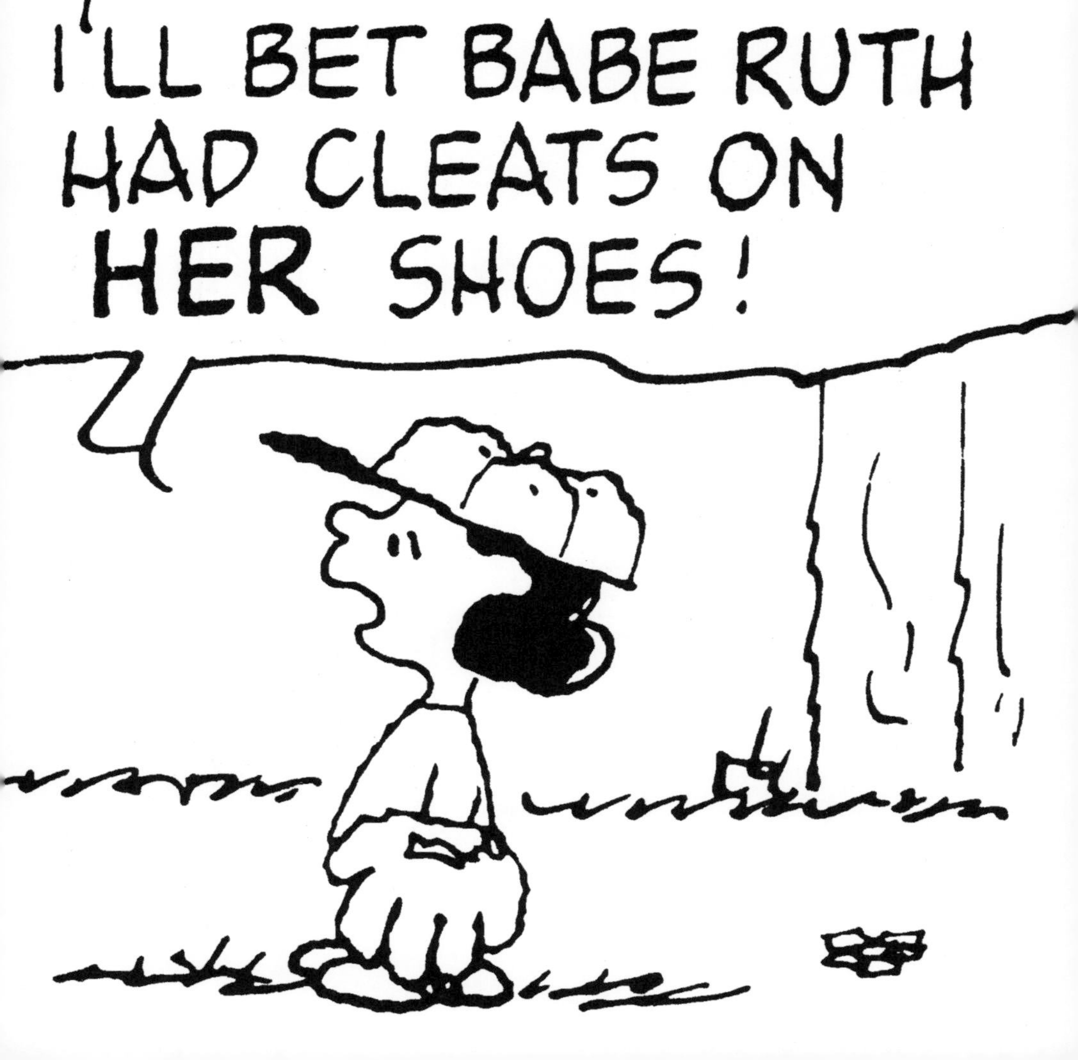
I'LL BET BABE RUTH HAD CLEATS ON HER SHOES!

Punt, Pass & Peanuts

Fans
&
Fanatics

Fans & Fanatics

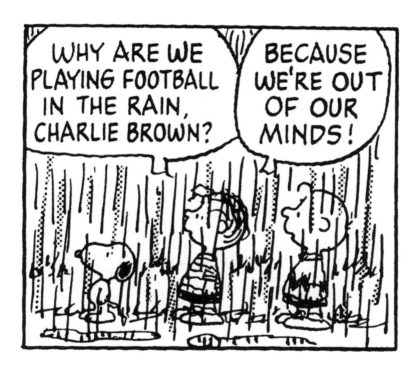

Play Rough
&
Hang Tough

Play Rough & Hang Tough

Sideline
Asides

Sideline Asides

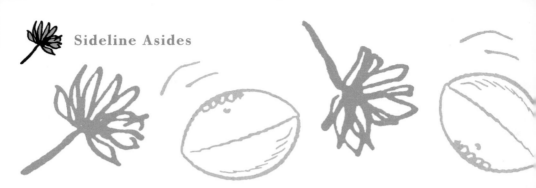

I'VE BEEN WATCHING AN EXCITING FOOTBALL GAME..THE CONGREGATION IS GOING WILD...

FOOTBALL GAMES HAVE FANS..CHURCHES HAVE CONGREGATIONS..CONCERTS HAVE AUDIENCES...

COURTROOMS HAVE SPECTATORS..RIOTS HAVE MOBS AND ACCIDENTS HAVE ONLOOKERS...

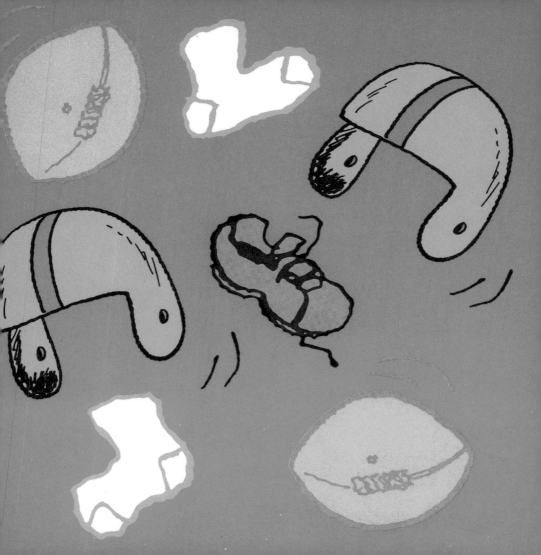